Painting

Glass Painting

Susie Johns

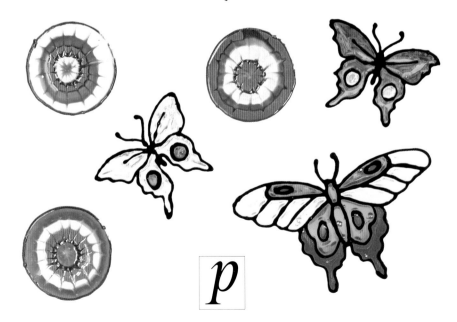

p

This is a Parragon Book

First published in 2002

Parragon
Queen Street House
4 Queen Street
Bath BA1 1HE, UK

Designed, produced and packaged by
Stonecastle Graphics Limited

Text and projects by Susie Johns
Design by Paul Turner and Sue Pressley
Photography by Roddy Paine
Edited by Philip de Ste. Croix

ISBN 0-75258-704-8

Printed in China

Acknowledgements:
The author would like to thank Pebeo for
providing some of the materials used in
making the projects.

Note:
Various glass art paints are available in
many colours from all good craft stores.

Contents

Introduction

The paints in your kit can be used to create motifs to decorate windows, mirrors and refrigerator doors.

Simply outline your chosen design on a sheet of plastic then fill in, using different coloured paints.

The squeezy bottles, with their fine nozzle tips, will allow you to create detailed patterns. The paint is bright and opaque when wet but dries to a flexible, transparent, plastic finish.

Leave your painted design to dry for approximately 24 hours, then peel it away from the backing. The motif will then cling to glass, metal and other shiny surfaces and can be peeled off and repositioned again and again.

Practise outlining on a spare sheet of plastic. Once you are confident, try this Celtic knot design from page 28. Wipe away any mistakes, as they occur, using a cotton bud. The outline can be filled in with red, yellow and blue paints.

Note:
The technique described here is ideal for beginners, and the paints and sheets of plastic in your kit can be used for many superb designs. You can start by following the easy projects on pages 8–11 before trying more advanced glass painting.

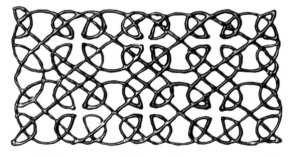

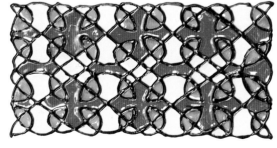

Painting on glass

You will need only a few specialist materials to start painting on glass. Begin with some pots of glass paint, one or two outliners and two soft paintbrushes – fine and medium.

Choose water-based paints, as these are safe to use, can be mixed to create a wide range of colours, and brushes can be cleaned easily with water and a little soap. Glass paints are available in transparent, opaque and frosted colours. With three pots of opaque glass paint – red, blue and yellow – you can mix shades of orange, purple and green. Transparent glass paints come in a wide range of beautiful colours and these can also be mixed together to make other colours.

Outliners are tubes of paste-like paint with a thin nozzle which helps to create a fine line. Black outliner can be used to create a basic design to fill in with colour, using transparent, frosted or opaque paints. Metallic outliners, available in silver, gold and pearlized colours, add a touch of sparkle while coloured outliners are slightly transparent.

Many everyday sauces and other food products are packaged in attractive jars and bottles. Bathroom toiletries are also often packaged in beautifully shaped glass containers. When they are empty, wash them thoroughly, remove the labels, and you instantly will have an interesting collection of items to decorate.

Some chocolates are packaged in clear plastic (acrylic) boxes, and so are CDs and tapes – these boxes have a lovely flat surface that's just right for painting. You can also buy sheets of acetate from craft shops, decorate them with glass paints and use them to make greetings cards, or cut them into small squares to make mosaics (see page 20).

Don't forget that you can use other things to decorate your projects too – try sticking on jewels or sequins, or thread beads onto wire and wrap these around bottle necks (see page 24) to make your glass art truly original.

Butterflies

Why not decorate a window with a group of these beautiful butterflies? You will find motifs to trace on page 30. Make several, in different shapes and colour combinations.

1 Place a plastic sheet over the butterfly motif. Use black paint to trace the outlines.

2 With yellow paint, fill in areas of the butterfly. Squeeze enough paint into each space to flood the area.

3 Now fill in the red areas of the design. Once more, squeeze out enough paint to fill the space completely, right up to the black lines.

4 Fill in remaining spaces with blue paint and leave for 24 hours to dry.

When the design is completely dry, simply peel it from the plastic backing and apply it to a window. The finished motif will cling to the glass and can be repositioned at any time.

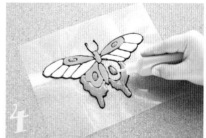

Psychedelic Swirls

While the glass paint is still wet it can be manipulated, creating swirling blends of colour. Try this technique on simple circles and squares, then use the motifs to decorate a mirror.

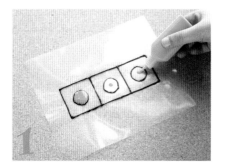

1 Draw a simple design of circles within squares, as shown. Trace the outlines using black paint then fill in each circle with a different colour. Add a spot of a contrasting colour in the centre of each.

2 Surround each circle with a contrasting colour, the fill in the remaining spaces within the squares with different colours.

3 While the paint is still wet, draw the pointed tip of a cocktail stick from the centre of each circle towards the outer edges of the squares, creating a psychedelic marbled effect.

Larger circles, outlined with black and filled with differently coloured rings, also look effective. When it comes to marbling, you can either draw the point of the cocktail stick from the centre towards the edge of the circle, or from the edge towards the centre. You can use a few of your completed motifs to jazz up a plain mirror.

Picture Border

Create a floral border design on a plain, inexpensive clip frame – an easy but effective transformation!

You will need:

- 18 cm x 12.5 cm clip frame
- transparent glass outliner in emerald green and turquoise blue
- transparent glass paints in lemon yellow, emerald green, rose pink and turquoise blue
- fine paintbrush

1 Remove the clips from the frame and place the glass over the border design on page 29. Use a ruler to draw border lines with green outliner.

2 Trace the stems and leaves with green outliner. Then trace the flowers with turquoise blue outliner. Leave to dry for about 1 hour.

3 Paint the areas between the lines with transparent glass paints, using a soft brush. Paint the background yellow, the leaves emerald green, the flower centres pink and petals turquoise blue.

When the paints are dry, place the glass on the backing board and replace the clips. You could add a favourite photograph to the centre of the frame, or simply sandwich a couple of leaves or flower petals between the glass and the backing board.

Top Tip

Make sure you wash your paintbrush immediately after using glass paints. If you use water-based paints, brushes are easily cleaned in soapy water. Do not let the paint harden on the brush.

Flower Basket

A square-sided bottle or vase provides an ideal flat surface for a detailed motif such as this basket of flowers.

You will need:

- chinagraph pencil
- glass outliner in pewter
- transparent glass paints in lemon yellow, golden yellow, red, emerald green and purple
- fine paintbrush

1 Trace the flower basket design from page 31 onto thin paper. Go over the outlines of the design on the reverse of the paper, using a chinagraph pencil.

2 Tape the paper to the bottle and go over the lines, transferring the design to the glass.

3 Remove the paper and go over the lines again, if necessary, using the chinagraph pencil. Apply pewter outliner to the lines and allow to dry. Remove any remaining traces of the pencil lines using a damp cotton bud.

4 Add colour to the motif – lemon yellow for the flower centres, a golden yellow for the basket and some of the flowers, red for flower petals, emerald green for leaves and stems. Paint the background with purple paint.

Other ideas

Make a greetings card by painting the design onto a sheet of acetate. You can lay the acetate directly over the design on page 31. Cut a rectangular aperture in the front of a piece of folded card and tape the completed design behind this 'window'.

Owl Jar

Any jar with a flat surface can be decorated with this motif, using a combination of transparent and opaque glass paints.

You will need:
- coffee jar
- glass outliner in black
- transparent glass paints in golden yellow and turquoise blue
- opaque glass paints in fuchsia and lime green
- fine paintbrush

1 Trace the owl motif from page 29 onto paper and tape it inside the jar. Use black outliner to trace the lines. Draw a border all round the design, following the shape of the jar.

2 Paint the leaves opaque green, the circles and the owl's body transparent yellow and the owl's wings and the flowers opaque fuchsia. Fill in the background with turquoise blue. Leave to dry.

Other ideas

Decorate a bottle in the same way, taping the design traced onto paper inside the bottle and tracing the lines with black outliner. In the picture opposite, the cockerel motif from page 31 has, like the owl, been painted using a combination of transparent and opaque colours.

Top Tip

It is important to degrease glass objects before painting them, to make sure the paint adheres to the surface. To do this, simply wash the glass jars or bottles that you are going to use in hot soapy water and dry them thoroughly.

Funky Fairies

Fill a frame with a hand-painted design. These funky fairies can be outlined in gold or silver, then painted with frosted glass paints. You can even add jewels to them for extra sparkle!

You will need:

- glass outliners in gold or silver
- frosted glass paints in rose, mauve and blue
- opaque glass paints in ivory, pink and yellow
- fine paintbrush
- small gemstones

1 Remove the acrylic panel from the frame and place it over the fairy motif on page 32. Trace the lines with gold outliner.
2 Add dots of outliner and press a small jewel into each one while it is still wet. Leave to dry.
3 Fill in the rest of the design using frosted glass paints – rose, mauve and blue. For face and arms, mix ivory, pink and yellow together to make a skin tone.

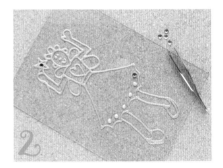

Top Tip

Frosted glass paints are semi-transparent, with a shimmery quality, ideal for this project. You could, however, use transparent or opaque glass paints, if you preferred.

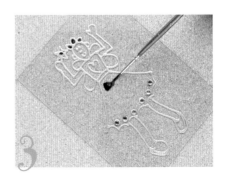

Mosaic Boxes

Collect acrylic boxes and decorate them with translucent mosaic patterns.

You will need:
- clear acrylic box
- transparent glass paints in golden yellow, turquoise blue, purple, fuchsia, red and blue
- six A5 sheets of clear acetate
- broad, flat, soft paintbrush
- clear crystal gel

1 Paint each sheet of acetate a different colour, using broad brushstrokes all in one direction. Leave to dry, flat.

2 Cut each sheet into 1 cm strips, then each strip into 1 cm squares. Coat the lid of the box with a thick layer of gel.

3 Quickly arrange squares into a pattern, pressing them into the wet gel. Repeat with the sides of the box. Leave to dry.

Top Tip

Chocolates, sweets and some bath products are often packed in transparent plastic boxes, which are ideal for decorating with glass paints. Carefully peel off any labels, removing any sticky residue with soapy water, and make sure the surface is really clean, dry and grease-free before you start painting.

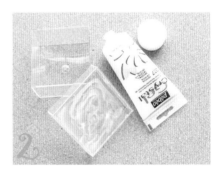

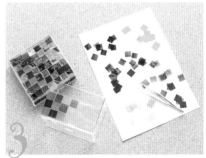

 Herb Jars

Decorate a set of small jars with leafy designs, painted freehand. Fine details can be scratched into the paint when dry.

You will need:
- set of small glass jars
- transparent glass paint in dark green
- fine paintbrush
- needle

1 Using dark green transparent glass paint and a fine, soft brush, paint different leaf shapes on each jar. Leave to dry. Then, using a needle, scratch leaf veins in the dry paint. To make the designs permanent, bake the painted jars in an oven following the paint manufacturer's instructions.

Other ideas
A square-sided jar can be recycled to hold olive oil or salad dressing. Decorate it with a leafy motif with details scratched into the surface of the paint, as before.

Tea lights

Small glasses make lovely candle holders, especially when they are decorated with colourful transparent glass paints.

1 Simply paint coloured vertical stripes onto small, heavy glasses, using a medium-sized, soft paintbrush.

Place a tea light in each painted glass. The tea light holders look particularly effective arranged in a circle on a shiny plate or tray which will reflect the light.

Be safe: Remember to take care with all types of candles and never leave tea lights unattended when they are alight.

Dressing Table Set

Choose small bottles and jars with elegant shapes that will look good on your dressing table when you have completed them. Paint them all over with transparent colour then add some exotic decoration.

You will need:

- small jar or bottle
- transparent glass paints in turquoise blue, purple, blue and fuchsia
- glass outliners in silver and pearl
- medium paintbrush

1 Use a medium-sized brush with soft bristles to paint your bottle or jar all over with transparent colour. Load your brush with plenty of paint and make sure the brushstrokes all go in the same direction. Leave to dry.

2 With silver or pearl outliners, decorate the bottle all over with random squiggles. Wipe off any mistakes immediately, using a cotton bud. Leave to dry.

Other ideas

As well as squiggles, dots of outliner also look effective. Cover a faceted bottle with transparent paint in two contrasting colours, then add dots of paint along dividing lines.

A cork bottle stopper can be embellished with beads spiked on pins, which can be either plain or glass-headed.

Wrap bottle necks with glass beads threaded onto fine wire, or with short lengths of marabou feather trim.

Blue Moods

Blue glass, decorated with simple flowers, makes a lovely set for the bedside or the dining table…

You will need:

- blue glass bottles
- masking tape
- opaque glass paints in ivory, pink, yellow and blue
- sponge-tipped brush
- medium-sized paintbrush

1 To paint a neat stripe around the bottle, stick two strips of masking tape in place, one above the other. Paint the gap in between with ivory glass paint, using a wide, sponge-tipped brush.

2 When the paint is dry, carefully peel away the masking tape. Paint dots of yellow using the tip of the medium-sized paintbrush. Then paint flower petals around each dot, using pink and blue paint and the flat side of the bristles.

Other ideas

Paint glasses with flowers to make a co-ordinating set. Simply paint a random line of dots, then add petals in ivory or pink or orange, which will show up well against the blue glass.

Top Tip

Opaque glass paints are ideal for decorating coloured glass where transparent paints might not show up, and they lend themselves very well to freehand painting techniques.